Lanarkshire's Lost Railways

by
Gordon Stansfield

An ex Caledonian Jumbo passing Mossend Station in May 1958.

Acknowledgements

Many thanks to W.A.C. Smith for the use of pictures on the front and back cover, inside front cover, pages 1, 4, 5, 6, 7, 9, 20, 22, 24, 27, 28, 30, 32-35, 42, 44, 46, 50, 51, 52.

© 1997 Gordon Stansfield
First published in the United Kingdom, 1997
by Stenlake Publishing, Ochiltree Sawmill,
The Lade, Ochiltree, Ayrshire KA18 2NX
Tel/Fax (01290) 423114

ISBN 1 872074 96 0

Moss Lye signal box circa 1910.

Introduction

The earliest railways in Scotland were small waggon-ways mainly found at industrial sites like mines and ironworks. Primarily used for transporting charcoal, coal, ironstone or waste around the site or to the nearest river or canal, they were primitive and relied on horse or cable haulage.

By the mid 1820s a few small networks were beginning to appear, especially in Lanarkshire, Scotland's industrial heartland. Virtually all of these early railways were used primarily for freight traffic.

By the late 1830s a boom in construction culminated in the so called Railway Mania of 1844-45. Many hundreds of schemes were authorised by Parliament in this period; as many more were proposed but never built. This expansion saw the construction of the main lines from Edinburgh to Glasgow, the London to Edinburgh line and the main line to Aberdeen from Carlisle, as well as many smaller routes which criss-crossed the country.

Lanarkshire, with its many ironworks, coal and ironstone mines and its proximity to Glasgow, was well served by its older mineral railways as well as new routes. The railways were promoted as mineral lines; passenger traffic was a secondary concern. However, the companies soon realised its potential growth and very quickly catered for it.

By the mid 1860s, a myriad of small companies were beginning to be amalgamated to form larger groupings. The North British and Caledonian Railways started to gobble up some of the smaller lines and expanded quickly. The North British won control of the Edinburgh & Glasgow Railway, The Monkland Railway and other smaller lines while the Caledonian took control of the Scottish Central Railway, giving it control of a main line stretching from Carlisle to Aberdeen as well as many of the associated feeder lines. Small lines were promoted locally and were built by money provided by the local inhabitants but were unable to cope with the demands made on what was becoming a truly national railway system. Consequently, they were vulnerable to collapse or takeover mergers by the bigger players.

The mid 1870s saw further expansion as the larger companies competed with each other to fill in the gaps of areas covered and to gain market share. By the 1890s, some of the old mineral lines had outlived their usefulness as the concerns they served had closed down. By the turn of the century, the railway network was at its zenith with few new lines being built.

During World War One, the railways came under the effective control of the Government which realised that the many small companies in both Scotland and England should amalgamate further to make four large companies. The two major groupings which covered Scotland were the London & North Eastern Railway (formed out of the NBR and the Great North of Scotland Railway as well as some English companies) and the London, Midland & Scottish Railway (formed out of the Caledonian Railway, the Glasgow & South Western Railway, the Highland Railway and, again, some English companies). This grouping, which took place in 1923 saw a rationalisation of services and some lines were closed as a result. The two big railway companies also started operating bus services which hastened the demise of some of their own lines. Indeed, the LNER and LMS jointly owned a great part of the SMT bus group.

Again during World War Two, the Government took control of the railways and ran them for the duration. By the end of the war, the Labour Government had decided to nationalise the railways. A major rationalisation then took place. Both the LMS and LNER had inherited a legacy of duplicated railway lines and services. As they were still in competition with each other, many of these lines were still open when British Railways took over in 1948. Stations on main lines that were too far from the town or village they purported to serve, or were uneconomic to keep open, were closed. Many lines that had outlived their profitable years and were a declining source of revenue were also shut.

It is a myth that Dr Beeching was responsible for the loss of our lines and stations. Many were closed years before he took charge of the railways in the 1960s. He only dealt the final death knell for many of the uneconomic lines which were left. There have been few closures over the last ten or fifteen years and some lines and stations have even re-opened.

Unfortunately, the Government's privatisation of the railways promises to create a nightmare for any user of the system and recreates the situation of the 1850s. In a few years the railways may go from owning bus companies to being owned by privatised bus companies. Another rationalisation may lie ahead with the less profitable lines being supplanted by bus services instead.

Gordon Stansfield, April 1997.

Airdrie: Hallcraig Street – Greenside Junction

Passenger Service Withdrawn   December 1870
Distance   0.5 Miles
Company   North British

Station Closed
Hallcraig Street   December 1870

Services on this line began on 26th December 1844 under the ownership of the Ballochney Railway. At first the services ran from Hallcraig Street to an exchange platform situated at Bothlin Viaduct which was east of the present day Lenzie Station. This service involved trains running over the metals of the Monkland & Kirkintilloch Railway thereby allowing journeys to be made to and from Glasgow. In July 1847 through journeys were in operation between Hallcraig Street and Glasgow but these only lasted until 10th December 1851 when all passenger services over the Monkland & Kirkintilloch were withdrawn.

The Ballochney Railway became part of the Monkland Railway Company in August 1848. The latter was absorbed into the North British Railway on 1st August 1865.

Initially the operating gauge on the line was 4 feet 6 inches but it was converted to the standard gauge of 4 feet 8.5 inches in July 1847. With the rapid development of railways in the Monklands new patterns of services emerged resulting in the closure of Hallcraig Street in December 1870 although goods services continued until July 1964.

Airdrie North Goods Station, Hallcraig Street, October 1955.

Airdrie South – Ratho (Newbridge Junction)

Passenger Service Withdrawn	9th January 1956	*Stations Closed*	
Distance	25 Miles	Clarkston (Lanark)	9th January 1956
Company	North British	Plains	18th June 1951
		Caldercruix	9th January 1956
		Forrestfield	22nd September 1930

Plains Station December 1955.

Airdrie South – Ratho (Newbridge Junction)

This line was opened in stages with the Edinburgh & Glasgow Railway opening the first section from Ratho to Bathgate in November 1849. The Bathgate & Coatbridge Railway opened the remaining section into Coatbridge and forward into Glasgow. Services to Coatbridge began in August 1862. By April 1871 through services were in operation between Edinburgh and Glasgow.

Although passenger services were withdrawn on 9th January 1956, summer seasonal services operated to various holiday locations until 1960. The station at Airdrie South was renamed Airdrie and became the eastern terminus of the Glasgow North "Blue Trains". Passenger services were re-introduced when a new station was opened beyond Airdrie at Drumgelloch in the late 1980s. In the east a passenger service was reintroduced from Ratho to Bathgate, providing an Edinburgh – Bathgate service.

Other passenger lines which joined this line were: Bangour – Uphall (closed 4th May 1921); Blackston – Bathgate Upper and Morningside – Bathgate Upper (closed 1st May 1930).

Three stations on the line had different names at some stage in their life. Uphall was known as Houston until 1st August 1865 while Drumshoreland was known as Broxburn until May 1870. Clarkston (Lanark) was known as Clarkston until 8th June 1953.

Clarkston Station
September 1955.

Airdrie – Whifflet

Passenger Service Withdrawn	3rd May 1943	*Stations Closed*	
Distance	2.25 Miles	Airdrie	3rd May 1943
Company	Caledonian	Calder	3rd May 1943

The eastern extremity of the Caledonian's line from Glasgow. Closure still allowed for trains to travel as far as Whifflet as closure only truncated the line by 2.25 miles. Airdrie Station had sufferred an earlier loss of services with the closure in 1930 of the Airdrie-Newhouse line.

Both Airdrie and Calder Stations were closed as a wartime economy measure between January 1917 and March 1919.

In 1922 there were fourteen departures on weekdays and twelve on Saturdays from Airdrie. These joined the Glasgow Central low level line at Bridgeton and terminated at Partickhill or Maryhill Central. Journey time for the seventeen miles was just over an hour.

Airdrie continued as a goods station until 6th July 1964 while Calder retained a goods service till 3rd April 1967.

A derelict Calder Station, April 1955.

Bankend – Coalburn

Passenger Service Withdrawn	After July 1926	*Station Closed*	
Distance	0.5 Miles	Bankend	After July 1926
Company	Caledonian		

The platform at Bankend was used by workers at the nearby Dalquhand Quarry as well as to Bankend Colliery. Passenger trains from Coalburn Station, a half mile distant, had to travel to Bankend as there was no crossing loop at Coalburn to turn the engines. It was intended that this line was to join the Glasgow & South Western line at Muirkirk but the extension was never opened. The signal box at Bankend remained in use until 1942.

Looking along the line from Coalburn Station to Bankend Colliery, March 1997.

Blackwood – Blackwood Junction

Passenger Service Withdrawn 1st July 1905
Distance 0.5 Miles
Company Caledonian

Station Closed
Blackwood (first) 1st July 1905

Blackwood received its first passenger service on 1st December 1866 when a line to Stonehouse and Hamilton was opened. The first station was at the end of a short branch from Blackwood Junction. In the line's early days, horses were used to pull the railway coach the half mile to Blackwood Station if a locomotive was unavailable. With the expansion of lines in the Lanarkshire area by the Caledonian Railway in the late 1890s and early 1900s, a new Blackwood Station was sited on a through line.

Empty coaches at the original Blackwood Station in April 1962.

Blackwood Junction – Tillietudlum (Southfield Junction)

Passenger Service Withdrawn   1st October 1951
Distance   2 Miles
Company   Caledonian

This short branch linked the stations at Blackwood and Tillietudlum, the latter being on the Hamilton – Brocketsbrae line. Built in the early 1900s, the level of service over this two mile line was very limited. In 1922 only three passenger trains used the line and by 1949 there was only one service using the line.

The Hamilton – Brocketsbrae line closed on the same date but Blackwood continued to have a passenger service until the mid 1960s.

Tillietudlem Station 1906.

Bothwell (Bothwell Junction) – Coatbridge (Sunnyside Junction)

Passenger Service Withdrawn	10th September 1951
Distance	6.25 Miles
Company	North British
Stations Closed	
Bothwell Park	Not Known
Bellshill	10th September 1951
Whifflet (first)	29th June 1895
Whifflet	22nd September 1930
Coatbridge Central	10th September 1930

Opened in the early 1880s, the line was used mainly for freight traffic. Like other lines it had its service curtailed during World War One and was closed from 1st January 1917 until 2nd June 1919 except for the provision of workmens' trains. By 1922 the pattern of services had developed in such a way that trains ran from Hamilton along the line to Coatbridge then joined the North British line from Airdrie to Glasgow. Many trains continued on to Glasgow Queen Street Low Level Station. This pattern of service continued until closure. The line from Hamilton to Shettleston was closed the following year.

The station at Bothwell Park was used by miners and did not feature in the public timetable For a period in the 1940s some of the services which did not go past Coatbridge Central were operated by Sentinel railcars but by 1948 these services had reverted back to steam haulage.

The exterior of Coatbridge Central in the mid 1930s.

Bothwell – Fallside (Fallside Junction)

Passenger Service Withdrawn	5th June 1950
Distance	1 Mile
Company	Caledonian

Station Closed	
Bothwell	5th June 1950

Bothwell was one of several places in Scotland that could boast train services provided by more than one railway company. The Caledonian Railway's branch line ran from a rather grand station at Bothwell to Fallside Junction where it joined the main line between Glasgow Central and Carlisle. The other branch was operated by the North British Railway and ran from Hamilton through Bothwell to Shettleston where it joined the Airdrie – Glasgow line.

At one time competition between the two was rife. In 1922 each company provided services from Bothwell to Glasgow with a journey time of about half an hour for the ten mile journey. Caledonian trains arrived at Central Low Level while North British trains arrived at Queen Street Low Level.

From 1st January 1917 until 2nd June 1919 the line was closed to passenger traffic. The inroad made by the trams and then buses to Bothwell resulted in the demise of the service and by 1949 the pattern of services was very fragmented.

The Caledonian's Bothwell Station just behind the war memorial has now cleverly been adapted as a factory and some of the buildings still remain.

Bothwell – Shettleston (Shettleston Junction)

Passenger Service Withdrawn	4th July 1955	*Stations Closed*	
Distance	5.25 Miles	Bothwell	4th July 1955
Company	North British	Uddingston East	4th July 1955
		Uddingston West	4th July 1955
		Maryville	1st February 1908
		Broomhouse	24th September 1927
		Mount Vernon North	4th July 1955

Uddingston East Station circa 1910

Bothwell – Shettleston (Shettleston Junction)

This line formed the northern section of the North British route from Hamilton to Shettleston and opened for passenger traffic on 1st April 1878. The section from Hamilton to Bothwell was closed on 15th September 1952 due to the dangerous condition of a viaduct over the River Clyde. From 1st January 1919 until 2nd June 1919 all passenger services, apart from workmens' trains, were suspended. Maryville and Uddingston West were passenger only stations and never had any freight facilities.

With nationalisation, it was only a matter of time before name changes to stations in certain areas were sorted out. Uddingston East was known as Uddingston until September 1952 while Mount Vernon North was known as Mount Vernon until 28th February 1953. Freight services were withdrawn from Broomhouse Station on 1st September 1953 while Bothwell and Uddingston East lost their freight service on 6th June 1961.

Looking from Bothwell Station, March 1997.

Brocketsbrae – Ferniegair (Merryton Junction)

Passenger Service Withdrawn	1st October 1951	*Stations Closed*	
Distance	10 Miles	Brocketsbrae	1st October 1951
Company	Caledonian	Auchenheath	1st October 1951
		Tillietudlem	1st October 1951
		Netherburn	1st October 1951
		Dalserf	1st October 1951
		Larkhall East	1st October 1951

Passenger services began on 1st December 1866 between Brocketsbrae and Ferniegair but the intention was that trains would go to either Hamilton or Motherwell. This was achieved on 1st April 1868 when a line between Motherwell and Ferniegair was opened and in October 1876 when the line between Hamilton and Ferniegair was completed.

Brocketsbrae Station circa 1907

Brocketsbrae – Ferniegair (Merryton Junction)

The line was used mainly for coal and mineral traffic but always had a passenger service although traffic was sparse. At one time the line continued beyond Brocketsbrae towards Coalburn and Douglas but this service was withdrawn in September 1939. Services were suspended on the Alton Heights Junction – Brocketsbrae part of the route from January 1941 until May 1945. Two branches joined the Brocketsbrae to Ferniegair line. The branch from Dalserf to Stonehouse closed in January 1935 and the branch from Tillietudlem to Blackwood closed on 1st October 1951.

Tillietudlum was a favourite spot for excursions and in the summer months many Sunday school outings arrived there on special trains. The level of normal passenger services on the line was minimal and trains consisted of one or two coaches. In the last few years before closure there were only three arrivals and departures.

Brocketsbrae was known as Lesmahagow until June 1905 and Dalserf was known as Ayr Road until July 1903 and Larkhall East was known as Larkhall until June 1905.

Freight services to Brocketsbrae and Auchenheath lasted until September 1953, while those to Tillietudlem and Netherburn lasted till January 1960. Larkhall East closed for goods in December 1959 and Dalserf was shut in March 1964.

The Big Brig, Auchenheath.

Coalburn – Hamilton (Haughead Junction)

Passenger Service Withdrawn	4th October 1965	*Stations Closed*	
Distance	17.25 Miles	Coalburn	4th October 1965
Company	Caledonian	Bellfield Platform	1922
		Auchlochan Halt	After 1926
		Alton Heights Junction	After 1926
		Lesmahagow	4th October 1965
		Blackwood	4th October 1965
		Stonehouse	4th October 1965
		Larkhall	4th October 1965
		Ferniegair	1st January 1917

Looking from Larkhall Station to Ferniegair, March 1997.

Coalburn – Hamilton (Haughead Junction)

The Coalburn to Hamilton line was the last remaining route in this part of Lanarkshire as all the other branches had been progressively closed from the 1930s onwards. The line to Ferniegair and Hamilton via Brocketsbrae left this line at Alton Heights Junction and it was closed to passengers as far as Brocketsbrae in September 1939. Its remaining section from there to Hamilton lasted until 1951. At Stonehouse a branch ran to Strathaven Central and another to Darvel. The Darvel passenger service was withdrawn in January 1935 and that to Strathaven lasted until the same date as the Coalburn service.

There were three locations where trains stopped to set down or pick up workmen. These were Auchlochan Halt, Alton Heights Junction and Bellfield Platform. Beyond Coalburn an eight mile line was built to Muirkirk but never opened to traffic. The line was constructed in the 1880s to serve the surrounding area which was rich in coal deposits. Known as the Spyreslack branch, the line was signalled throughout and had extensive engineering works including three viaducts. Part of the line did open to serve Bankend Colliery and carried miners to the colliery. Muirkirk was in Glasgow & South Western territory and when the Caledonian learned that the Glasgow & South Western might seek running powers over it towards Hamilton they decided not to open the line. The track was lifted during the First World War.

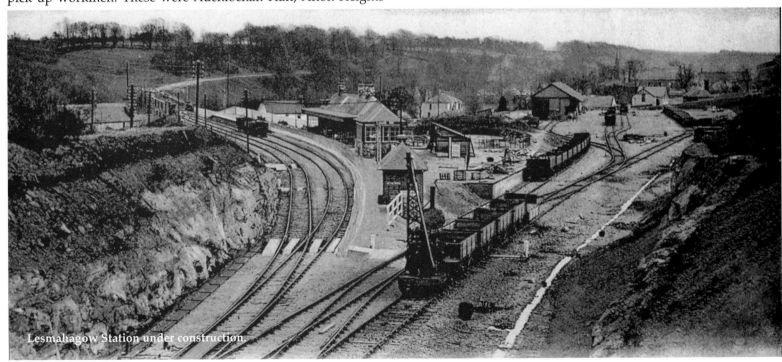

Lesmahagow Station under construction.

Coatbridge Central – Rutherglen (Rutherglen East Junction)

Passenger Service Withdrawn	7th November 1966
Distance	8.75 Miles
Company	Caledonian

Stations Closed

Langloan	5th October 1964
Drumpark	5th October 1964
Baillieston	5th October 1964
Calderpark Halt	4th July 1955
Mount Vernon South	16th August 1943
Carmyle	5th October 1964

Baillieston Station circa 1908

Coatbridge Central – Rutherglen (Rutherglen East Junction)

This is one of the few passenger lines on which a service has been re-introduced. Strathclyde Passenger Transport Executive re-instated train services and re-opened some of the stations along the line. The re-opening took place in late 1993 but instead of trains going to Coatbridge Central they now go to a new station at Whifflet on the line between Motherwell and Coatbridge.

Before the line closed, the pattern of services provided was very varied. In October 1964, along with the discontinuation of passenger services on the Glasgow Central low level lines, the local passenger service to Coatbridge was withdrawn. These services joined the Rutherglen – Coatbridge line at Carmyle after travelling from Bridgeton Cross and Parkhead Stadium.

The Coatbridge – Rutherglen line between Carmyle and Rutherglen had no passenger stations and tended only to carry through passenger trains. Up until November 1966 the only scheduled passenger train was the southbound "Royal Highlander" from Inverness to London Euston.

Drumpark and Calderpark Halt had no freight facilities and the latter was near Glasgow Zoo. The last passenger timetable for the line showed five to six weekday journeys in both directions between Glasgow and Coatbridge.

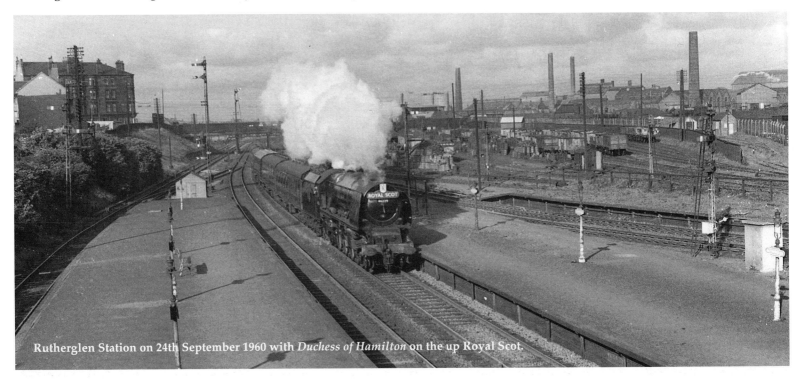

Rutherglen Station on 24th September 1960 with *Duchess of Hamilton* on the up Royal Scot.

Dolphinton – Carstairs (Dolphinton Junction)

		Stations Closed	
Passenger Service Withdrawn	2nd June 1945	Dolphinton	2nd June 1945
Distance	10.75 Miles	Dunsyre	2nd June 1945
Company	Caledonian	Newbigging	2nd June 1945
		Bankhead	2nd June 1945

The village of Dolphinton was on the border between the counties of Lanarkshire and Peebleshire. Here the metals of two railway companies – the Caledonian from Carstairs and the North British from Leadburn near Edinburgh – also met. Each company had its own railway station at Dolphinton although the service from Leadburn ceased in 1933. The Caley line opened in 1867. The service was typically rural and in 1922 there were three return journeys to Carstairs with the eleven mile journey taking about half an hour.

Even in 1922 there were no through trains along the line with passengers having to rebook at the relevant Dolphinton Station and in many instances wait a while for a connection. The line was temporarily closed from 12th September 1932 until 17th July 1933. Freight services lasted until November 1950.

Dunsyre Station circa 1907.

Douglas West (Poniel Junction) – Brocketsbrae

Passenger Service Withdrawn   11th September 1939
Distance   4 Miles
Company   Caledonian

Poniel Junction was the branch of three routes – south to Muirkirk, north east to Lanark and north west to Brocketsbrae and Hamilton. The main reason for the existence of the line was to allow freight traffic to be brought through Brocketsbrae towards Muirkirk avoiding the need for these trains to go via Carstairs which was subject to very heavy traffic demands at peak periods.

Opened in 1883 as the Muirkirk & Lesmahagow Junction Railway, the passenger service provided was very limited. In 1922 there were two trains to Douglas West from Brocketsbrae. These trains required the engine to be changed from one end to the other in order to complete the journey after reaching Poniel Junction.

The line closed to freight traffic in 1954.

2-6-4T no.42204 at Douglas West with the 6.30pm to Lanark, 1st October 1960.

East Kilbride – Blantyre (Hunthill Junction)

Passenger Service Withdrawn	14th July 1924	*Station Closed*	
Distance	3.5 Miles	Calderwood Glen Platform	September 1939
Company	Caledonian		

Running eastwards from East Kilbride towards Hamilton this route joined the Hamilton to Strathaven line at High Blantyre. Opened in 1883 by the Caledonian Railway the line never lived up to its expectations. Its route was lightly populated and as a result traffic was sparse. The line closed at first on 1st October 1914 when there were two to four trains daily. Services were re-instated on 1st October 1923 when one passenger train per week used the line but this service lasted less than a year and the service was finally withdrawn on 14th July 1924.

There was an intermediate platform at Calderwood Glen which served a local beauty spot. Opened in 1907, no scheduled trains called as it was served by excursion trains from Glasgow and the Motherwell/Hamilton area. The last train to visit here was in September 1939.

High Blantyre Station circa 1910.

Ferniegair – Hamilton (Ross Junction)

Passenger Service Withdrawn	2nd October 1876	*Station Closed*	
Distance	1 Mile	Ferniegair (First)	2nd October 1876
Company	Caledonian		

80110 approaching Ferniegair Junction in July 1960 with an Orange Walk special to Larkhall. The line from Ross Junction is on the left.

When a new direct line between Ferniegair and Hamilton opened in 1876, this short stretch of line was closed to passengers although it remained open to freight traffic until July 1964. The line had carried passenger traffic for just ten years, handling trains on the service from Hamilton to Brocketsbrae and Stonehouse.

Hamilton – Bothwell

Passenger Service Withdrawn	15th September 1952	*Stations Closed*	
Distance	2.5 Miles	Hamilton	15th September 1952
Company	North British	Peacock Cross	1st January 1917
		Burnbank	15th September 1952

The North British station in Hamilton was the third station in the town with the other two belonging to the Caledonian Railway. The section of line from Hamilton to Bothwell was opened to passenger traffic in April 1878. It was temporarily closed between January 1917 and June 1919 to all passenger traffic except for workmens' trains. Householders at Hamilton objected to the railway as they had no wish to see a railway station from their villas and demanded that the North British plant trees in order to screen the railway line and station.

The line was cut back to Bothwell in 1952 due to the dangerous condition of a viaduct over the River Clyde. However, services continued from Bothwell to Shettleston until 1955. At Bothwell there was a line to Coatbridge which had a passenger service until September 1951.

Burnbank Station circa 1906.

High Blantyre (Auchenraith Junction) – Blantyre (Blantyre Junction)

Passenger Service Withdrawn   30th September 1945
Distance   2 Miles
Company   Caledonian

This short spur left the Strathaven – Hamilton West line before it reached Hamilton West Station. The spur headed westwards to reach Blantyre Station forming the third side of a triangular junction. The trains which used the line mainly originated at Strathaven with some continuing to Hamilton West while others went to Blantyre. When the service from Hamilton West to Strathaven was withdrawn in September 1945 the service to Blantyre from Strathaven was also withdrawn.

Blantyre Station about 1910.

Holytown (Holytown South Junction) – Wishaw (Wishaw Central Junction)

Passenger Service Withdrawn   19th August 1962
Distance   3 Miles
Company   Caledonian

This route linked two lines which are still in use today. At Wishaw it connected with the west coast main line and at Holytown with the Glasgow – Edinburgh route via Shotts. Opened in 1850, the pattern of service over the line was very infrequent with most trains running between Holytown and Wishaw.

The last passenger services on the line were through express services which ran on summer saturdays only. These originated at Law Junction Station and were departures to the Ayrshire coast.

Class 5 no.45706 passing Jenny Lind Siding with the afternoon fish train from Aberdeen to London on 18th March 1963.

Kirkhill (Kirkhill Junction) – Carmyle (Westburn Junction)

Passenger Service Withdrawn 17 June 1957
Distance 1 Mile
Company Caledonian

Kirkhill, on the south eastern outskirts of Glasgow, is the last station before Newton Junction is reached on the route to Cathcart. The link ran northwards, joining the Newton – Carmyle line at Westburn Junction before it became part of the Glasgow Central low level system. Although the line was fairly short it had two impressive viaducts, one of which crossed over the west coast main line.

This line could have formed a circular service around the south east of Glasgow but it never really became a true suburban route, and by 1949 there was only one service running. After the line was closed to passenger traffic it was used as carriage sidings for the Kirkhill services before finally closing in August 1966.

The Clyde Viaduct at Westburn Junction with 2-6-4T no.42208 on a parcels run from Hamilton on 15th August 1963.

Lanark (Silvermuir South Junction) – Carstairs (Lanark Junction)

Passenger Service Withdrawn   18th April 1966
Distance   0.5 Miles
Company   Caledonian

This short spur linked the west coast main line at Lanark Junction with the line which is still in use today from Lanark. It allowed trains to run between Edinburgh and Lanark as well as some local services from Carlisle. When these services were withdrawn there was no need to retain the spur for passenger use.

Lanark is still served today by electric trains from Glasgow Central with the section of line to Lanark from the main line being single. When the line from Dalreoch to Balloch Central was singled the surplus overhead line and gantries were used to electrify the Lanark branch.

Snow clearing in January 1913.

Manuel Low Level – Coatbridge Sunnyside (Greenside Junction)

Passenger Service Withdrawn	1st May 1930	*Stations Closed*	
Distance	17 Miles	Longriggend	1st May 1930
Company	North British	Arbuckle	October 1862
		Whiterigg	1st May 1930
		Rawyards	1st May 1930
		Commonhead (Airdrie North)	1st May 1930

This route ran from Coatbridge Sunnyside (on the present day Glasgow North Suburban line) to Manuel Low Level Station. The line continued northwards from Manuel to reach the ex-NBR port of Bo'ness. The service between these two locations lasted till 1934.

Built to link the industrial heartland of North Lanarkshire with Bo'ness, the line was fairly steeply graded at several locations and had quite a number of intermediate stations. The journey time for the sixteen mile trip was just over an hour in the mid 1920s with four return trips on weekdays.

Freight services were withdrawn from the intermediate stations at various times between 1930 and 1964. The line was frequently used for Railtour specials over the years.

Rawyards Station in a state of dereliction, October 1955.

Morningside – Carfin (Cleland Junction)

		Stations Closed	
Passenger Service Withdrawn	1st December 1930		
Distance	5.5 Miles	Morningside (first)	February 1853
Company	Caledonian	Morningside	1st December 1930
		Davies Dyke	April 1848
		Newmains	1st December 1930
		Cleland	1st December 1930

Lasting seven months longer than the North British service from Bathgate to Morningside, this line headed west and joined the present day Edinburgh – Glasgow via Shotts line at Carfin.

In the mid 1920s there were four trains daily with an additional journey on saturdays. Most trains continued to Holytown. The line was closed to pasengers for reasons of wartime economy from January 1917 until June 1919 and freight services along the line lasted until 1951.

The viaduct at Cleland.

Mossend : North Junction – Fullwood Junction

Passenger Service Withdrawn   5th November 1962
Distance   0.5 Miles
Company   Caledonian

Jubilee no.45738 Samson coming off the spur from Mossend at Fullwood Junction with the fish train from Aberdeen. The leading coaches are part of the Royal Train returning south on 9th August 1963.

This short spur at Mossend linked the Coatbridge Central – Motherwell line with the Edinburgh – Glasgow via Shotts line. The passenger service which used this line ran in its last days from Coatbridge Central to Holytown. At one time services had continued from Hamilton to Coatbridge and onwards to Glasgow Buchanan Street. When the local passenger service was withdrawn between Hamilton and Coatbridge no further passenger services used the spur. Whifflet Lower, on the line between Hamilton and Coatbridge, was re-opened by Strathclyde Passenger Transport Executive in December 1992. It formed part of the electrified service from Motherwell to Coatbridge Central as well as being used for the re-opened service from Glasgow Central to Coatbridge via Baillieston.

Muirkirk – Lanark (Smyllum West Junction)

Passenger Service Withdrawn	5th October 1964	*Stations Closed*	
Distance	18.75 Miles	Inches	5th October 1964
Company	Glasgow & South Western/	Douglas West	5th October 1964
	Caledonian	Happendon	5th October 1964
		Ponfeigh	5th October 1964
		Sandilands	5th October 1964
		Lanark Race Course Halt	5th October 1964

Sandilands on 1st October 1960 with the 1.16pm Lanark to Ponfeigh service.

Muirkirk – Lanark (Smyllum West Junction)

This was the easterly section of the route which ran from Ayr and allowed through trains to run between Ayrshire and Edinburgh. The first through trains to Muirkirk began in June 1874. Just past Muirkirk was a junction which formed a route to Coalburn. Known as the Spyreslack branch, the Caledonian built this line but never brought it into use as they feared that the Glasgow & South Western would seek running powers over it.

With the decline in coal and mineral traffic in the early part of the 20th century, the traffic generated from Muirkirk and other places along the line declined. A passenger service was maintained right up until 1964. Only one station, Happenden, had a name change and was known as Douglas until April 1931. There was a branch to Hamilton via Brocketsbrae.

Lanark Race Course Halt was an un-timetabled halt and handled not only race specials but also traffic to the Lanark Aviation Meeting of 6th-13th August, 1910. The last passenger timetable for the line gave five return trips between Lanark and Muirkirk on weekdays.

The same loco (45309) at Ponfeigh with the 2.27pm to Muirkirk on 1st October 1960.

Newhouse – Airdrie (North Junction)

Passenger Service Withdrawn	1st December 1930	*Stations Closed*	
Distance	3.5 miles	Newhouse	1st December 1930
Company	Caledonian	Chapelhall	1st December 1930
		Calderbank	1st December 1930

Opened in July 1888, this line provided a further inroad into the county of Lanarkshire by the Caledonian. The passenger service only ran between Newhouse and Airdrie although the railway line extended southwards from Newhouse to join the present-day Glasgow – Edinburgh via Shotts line. At Airdrie, the northern terminus, connections were available to Glasgow. The Caledonian station was the terminus of services from Glasgow to Coatbridge and Airdrie via Rutherglen. These continued until 1943 when the services were cut back to Whifflet.

The three and three quarter mile trip from Newhouse to Airdrie took about a quarter of an hour and, allowing for connections, Glasgow could be reached in an hour. Thirty two years after closure, the Newhouse Station buildings were still standing when a special visited the line in June 1962.

The last passenger train at Newhouse, a railtour special on 9th June 1962 hauled by ex Caley locomotive no. 57581.

Stonehouse (Stonehouse North Junction) – Dalserf (Stonehouse Junction)

Passenger Service Withdrawn	7th January 1935		*Station Closed*	
Distance	3.25 Miles		Stonehouse (first)	1st July 1905
Company	Caledonian			

This was one of the Caledonian's many lines in Lanarkshire and linked the route from Ferniegair to Strathaven with the Ferniegair – Brocketsbrae route. The line between Stonehouse and Dalserf formed part of the original route to Strathaven. However, when a shorter route opened in the early part of this century the line only saw the odd passenger train. The station at Stonehouse was resited on the shorter branch. In 1922 there was only one train in each direction between Stonehouse and Dalserf.

The viaduct at Stonehouse in 1904.

Stonehouse – Strathaven Central

Passenger Service Withdrawn	4th October 1965	*Station Closed*	
Distance	3.75 Miles	Strathaven Central	4th October 1965
Company	Caledonian		

Strathaven Central Station on opening day, 1st October 1904.

Stonehouse – Strathaven Central

This was the last route to reach Strathaven. The line from Stonehouse continued westwards to reach Darvel and Kilmarnock and joined the Glasgow & South Western line at County Boundary Junction. The service to Darvel was withdrawn in 1939. To the north was a line to Hamilton and Bothwell but this service was withdrawn in 1945.

The line opened in 1904 and in the mid 1920s there were about five arrivals and departures between Strathaven Central, Stonehouse and Hamilton. Hamilton could be also reached by trains from Glassford.

At Stonehouse, which was a junction station with three through platforms, there was a line to Blackwood and Coalburn which closed at the same time as the Stonehouse – Strathaven service. Strathaven Central was renamed Strathaven just four months before closure.

Strathaven Central, derelict and abandoned, March 1997.

Strathaven Central – Darvel

Passenger Service Withdrawn	11th September 1939	
Distance	10.5 Miles	
Company	Caledonian Glasgow & South Western	

Stations Closed

Ryeland	11th September 1939
Drumclog	11th September 1939
Loudoun Hill	11th September 1939

Opened on 1st May 1905, this line was known as the Strathaven and Darvel Railway. Great plans had been made for this line as it was envisaged as providing a new through route between Lanarkshire and Ayrshire. It all came to nothing as there was very little traffic along the route. Local services were poorly patronised simply because the area's population was small.

The three stations on the route were all closed from September until November 1909 and again from Janaury 1917 until December 1922. Services ran to Darvel from Kilmarnock until April 1964. Although the last passenger service ran on 10th September 1939 the actual official closure date was two weeks later. Freight services were withdrawn at the same time.

**Loudon Hill
Station circa 1908**

Strathaven Central – Hamilton (Strathaven Junction)

Passenger Service Withdrawn	30th September 1945	*Stations Closed*	
Distance	11.25 Miles	Strathaven North	30th September 1945
Company	Caledonian	Glassford	30th September 1945
		Quarter	30th September 1945
		Meikle Earnock Halt	12th December 1943
		High Blantyre	30th September 1945

Strathaven North circa 1910.

Known as the Hamilton & Strathaven Railway, this was originally a mineral line serving the coal mines above Hamilton. It was only at a later stage when a passenger service was envisaged that it was discovered that to arrive at Hamilton trains would have to double back at Haughead Junction. Passenger services began in February 1863. Most trains went to Strathaven North Station before continuing on their way to the new Strathaven Central Station which opened in 1904. The twelve mile trip took about forty minutes and there were about six return journeys daily.

The original Strathaven station closed in 1904. Freight services along the line lasted until 1953.

Strathaven (First) – Strathaven (Whiteshawgate Junction)

Passenger Service Withdrawn	30th September 1945	*Station Closed*	
Distance	0.75 Miles	Strathaven	1st October 1904
Company	Caledonian		

Strathaven's original station was part of the Hamilton & Strathaven Railway and opened to passenger traffic in February 1863. Unfortunately, the Strathaven terminus was about half a mile short of the town. It was not until 1904 that an extension was built in order to join the newly constructed line from Stonehouse to Strathaven at a new station called Strathaven Central. The original Strathaven Station was then closed.

One of the features of this short extension were the twin viaducts just outside Strathaven Central Station, each one carrying a different line.

The Pomillion Viaducts at Strathaven circa 1915.

Symington (Symington Junction) – Peebles

Passenger Service Withdrawn	5th June 1950	*Stations Closed*	
Distance	19 Miles	Coulter	5th June 1950
Company	Caledonian	Biggar	5th June 1950

The line between Symington and Peebles opened to passenger traffic in 1864. Peebles was in North British territory and although the two stations were linked by rail each was situated on a different side of the River Tweed and joined by a single connecting bridge. There were five trains in each direction with the journey taking about three quarters of an hour. In the early part of this century a special line was constructed in connection with work on Talla Reservoir. After the passenger service was withdrawn, freight services continued as far as Biggar and Broughton until 1966. The Caledonian station at Peebles was subsequently renamed Peebles West and the North British, Peebles East. After closure a school train continued to run to and from Biggar until the end of the school term. In the morning it ran from Symington to Biggar while in the afternoon it left Biggar at 16.03, joining the west coast main line at Symington before continuing south to Elvanfoot.

Coulter Station, August 1955.

Wanlockhead – Elvanfoot (Elvanfoot Junction)

Passenger Service Withdrawn	2nd January 1939	*Stations Closed*	
Distance	7.25 Miles	Wanlockhead	2nd January 1939
Company	Caledonian	Leadhills	2nd January 1939

The Caledonian Railway decided to obtain its first Light Railway Order in order to build a branch line from Elvanfoot (on the main west coast line) to Wanlockhead.

The line was opened throughout in October 1902. It required some fairly difficult engineering works and featured two notable viaducts.

Wanlockhead and Leadhills were very scenic villages and attracted a large number of tourists in the summer months. The maximum speed on the line was 20mph and most passenger trains also carried freight. Leadhills was famous for its lead mines and deposits but this traffic declined with the liquidation of the Wanlockhead Mining Company in 1936.

In 1935, the London, Midland & Scottish Railway introduced a railcar service on sundays for ramblers. Normal service on the railway was four trains daily in each direction and the seven mile trip took forty minutes. Many remains of the railway can be seen today and there is now a new narrow guage railway at the mining museum at Wanlockhead.

Leadhills Railway Station in 1905.

Whifflet Upper – Langloan West Junction

Passenger Service Withdrawn	5th October 1964	*Station Closed*	
Distance	1 Mile	Whifflet Upper	5th October 1964
Company	Caledonian		

Whifflet Upper was known as Whifflet High Level until November 1953. It was, at the time of closure, the end of the line for some of the Glasgow suburban services to Carmyle, Baillieston and Coatbridge. The line beyond Whifflet closed several years earlier and had gone to Airdrie and Newhouse.

A re-opened Whifflet Station is now in use providing services to Motherwell, Coatbridge Central, Baillieston, and Glasgow Central High Level via Carmyle.

Looking from Whifflet Lower in the 1930s. The line to the left joined with the line to Whifflet Upper. A goods train is on the bridge and about to pass through Whifflet Upper which was located just off picture to the right.

Wilsontown – Auchengray (Wilsontown Junction)

Passenger Service Withdrawn   10th September 1951
Distance   3.5 Miles
Company   Caledonian

Stations Closed
Wilsontown   10th September 1951
Haywood   10th September 1951

Constructed primarily for freight traffic this line, like many other routes, did have a passenger service. The line from Wilsontown joined the Carstairs Junction – Edinburgh Princes Street route at Auchengray. The line extended beyond Wilsontown to Climpey Colliery. The journey took about ten minutes and up until closure there were about ten return trips daily.

Wilsontown Station circa 1908.

Wishaw Central – Cambusnethan

Passenger Service Withdrawn	1st January 1917	*Station Closed*	
Distance	1.5 Miles	Cambusnethan	1st January 1917
Company	Caledonian		

This line formed part of the route which linked Wishaw with Newmains. By reversing at Newmains a connection could be made to Morningside. It opened in 1901 and by 1909 the section from

Cambusnethan to Newmains had lost its passenger service. It was only a question of time before the remaining section lost its service with this happening in 1917.

Clan MacKintosh at Wishaw Central with a train from Glasgow Central to Lockerbie.

Carstairs – Edinburgh *(line still open)*

Carnwath, Auchengray and Cobbinshaw Stations were all closed on the 18th of April 1966 as part of the winding down of British Rail's unprofitable operations. This was the Caledonian's route to Edinburgh from the west coast main line and in 1888 the great railway races were run over the line. In a bid to attract both traffic and publicity, the east and west coast railways partook in furious races to Edinburgh in July and August of that year. The Caledonian entrusted one of their newest locos, no.123, to the task of running the Edinburgh portion of the west coast line's express from Euston. With her light load of only 105 tons she was extremely quick and reached a peak of 74mph on the 9th of August at Harburn.

Carnwath Station in 1910 with a goods train being unloaded.

Carstairs – Edinburgh *(line still open)*

The 1888 railway races were only to Edinburgh, but by 1895 the North British Railway had opened its two bridges over the Forth and Tay and the scene was set for an even greater race to Aberdeen. Traditionally there was a great exodus to Scotland during late July and August for the grouse shooting and the trains going to the north would be full of prestigious and important passengers. Whichever line won would take much of the traffic for the rest of the year. After a few weeks of heated racing, both sides called a day as speeds were becoming reckless and those passengers who had arrived in Aberdeen at the early hours of the morning had nowhere to go. In the end passenger patterns did not change and the races had acheived nothing.

Cobbinshaw Station circa 1910.

Gretna Junction – Glasgow (via Carstairs) *(line still open)*

1965 was a bad year for the west coast main line when ten stations between Elvanfoot and Glasgow lost their rail services as part of a rationalisation by British Railways. They were Elvanfoot, Crawford, Abington, Lamington, Symington, Thankerton, Gleghorn, Law Junction, Flemington and Eglinton Street.

Some stations lost services earlier including Braidwood in 1862, Wishaw South in 1958 and Fallside in 1953.

Flemington Station circa 1904.

Gretna Junction – Glasgow (via Carstairs) *(line still open)*

Construction of the Caledonian's main line began in 1845 and by 1847 over 20,000 navvies were engaged in construction. The line was opened soon after. When it was authorised, the west coast main line was one of the largest engineering projects ever given the green light by Parliament and ran through some of the most inhospitable country in Britain. Nowadays it has lost many of its feeder lines and most of its country stations.

Elvanfoot Station in 1963.

Motherwell – Coatbridge *(line still open)*

Many of the early mineral lines were first built in the Coatbridge area and grew to become main lines for both the Caley and North British. Railways arrived in Coatbridge and Whifflet to serve the expanding iron works and coal mines and by the mid 1830s there were numerous lines including the Wishaw and Coltness which ran from Whifflet to Motherwell. The original gauge of many of these mineral lines was 4ft 6" but they were soon converted to standard gauge. For Caledonian trains coming from the south, Whifflet was the junction for trains to the north and to Glasgow. To travel to the north, they had to exercise running powers over a short section of North British line.

Whifflet Lower Station with 2-6-4T no. 42206 on 14th August 1961.

Springburn – Cumbernauld *(line still open)*

Station Closed

Robroyston	11th June 1956
Stepps	5th November 1962
Garnkirk	7th March 1960
Gartcosh	5th November 1962
Glenboig	11th June 1956

On this line, Stepps Station, now known as Stepps Road, re-opened to passenger traffic on 16th May 1990.

Gartcosh Station in April 1962.